# STOP!

**This is the back of the book.**
**You wouldn't want to spoil a great ending!**

**This book is printed "manga-style," in the authentic Japanese right-to-left format. Since none of the artwork has been flipped or altered, readers get to experience the story just as the creator intended. You've been asking for it, so TOKYOPOP® delivered: authentic, hot-off-the-press, and far more fun!**

## DIRECTIONS

**If this is your first time reading manga-style, here's a quick guide to help you understand how it works.**

**It's easy... just start in the top right panel and follow the numbers. Have fun, and look for more 100% authentic manga from TOKYOPOP®!**

Marmalade
Boy

Vol. 1

By

Wataru Yoshizumi

Los Angeles • Tokyo • London

Story and Art - Wataru Yoshizumi
Translator - Jack Niida
English Adaptation - Jake Forbes
Retouch and Lettering - Carol Conception and Jinky DeLeon
Graphic Designer - Anna Kernbaum
Editor - Stephanie Donnelly
Associate Editors - Robert Coyner, Paul Morrisey

Senior Editor - Jake Forbes
Reprint Editor - Mark Paniccia
Managing Editor - Jill Freshney
Production Coordinator - Antonio DePietro
Production Manager - Jennifer Miller
Art Director - Matt Alford
Editorial Director - Jeremy Ross
VP of Production - Ron Klamert
President & C.O.O. - John Parker
Publisher & C.E.O. - Stuart Levy

Email: editor@TOKYOPOP.com
Come visit us online at www.TOKYOPOP.com

A TOKYOPOP® Manga

TOKYOPOP Inc.
5900 Wilshire Blvd. Suite 2000
Los Angeles, CA 90036



ISBN: 1-931514-54-2

First TOKYOPOP printing: March 2002
15 14 13 12 11 10 9 8 7 6
Printed in the USA

MIKI...
YOUR FATHER AND I HAVE SOMETHING TO TELL YOU.
WE'RE GETTING...
...DIVORCED. ♡
MOM AND DAD
ARE SPLITTING UP?

WHA...
WHAT DO YOU MEAN...
CRASH
AND THAT...
...DIVORCED?!
...WAS HOW MY LIFE GOT TURNED UPSIDE DOWN.

Year 1 Class B
THEY JUST SMILED AND SAID THEY'RE GETTING DIVORCED?
THAT'S AMAZING.
CAN YOU BELIEVE THEY EVEN USED A "♡" MARK AT THE END OF THEIR SENTENCE?!
MUNCH
MUNCH
IT'S JUST TOO MUCH!
I KNEW SOMETHING WAS UP WHEN I NOTICED THEM DRINKING FROM THE SPECIAL TEA SET,
BUT DIVORCE...?!
HOW COULD THIS HAPPEN? YOUR PARENTS SEEMED SO HAPPY TOGETHER.
JUST LAST MONTH, THE TWO OF THEM LEFT ON THAT ROMANTIC TRIP TO HAWAII.

YEAH,
THAT HAWAIIAN VACATION...
THAT'S WHY ALL THIS IS HAPPENING!
THE MATSUURAS ?!
WHO THE HECK ARE HEY?!
THEY WERE ON THE SAME HAWAIIAN TOUR AS US.
WE WERE ALL THE SAME AGE, SO WE REALLY TOOK TO EACH OTHER.
AS WE TRAVELED, I FELL IN LOVE WITH CHIYAKO AND YOUR MOTHER FELL IN LOVE WITH YOUJI.
YOU KNOW HOW THESE THINGS GO.
IN...
...LOVE?!
YUP.
SO, WE DISCUSSED THE SITUATION ND CONCLUDED THAT WE SHOULD ALL CHANGE ARTNERS AND REMARRY.

SHOCK
CHANG
PARTNERS...?!
NO WAY!
YOU TWO HAVE GOT TO BE KIDDING ME!
THAT'S THE CRAZIEST THING I'VE HEARD OF IN MY ENTIRE LIFE!!
I GUESS IT IS KIND-OF, WELL, UNUSUAL.
BUT, IT'S HAPPEN-ING NOW.
IT'S NOT THAT WE DON'T LOV EACH OTHE BUT IT'S N LONGER A PASSIONAT LOVE.
WHAT WE HAVE NOW IS MORE OF A... FRIENDLY LOVE.
UH-HUH. WE WERE FRIENDS FIRST, AND LOVERS SECOND, BEFORE WE GOT MARRIED, TOO.
WHA- WHAT ARE YOU SAYING?
EVEN IF THERE IS NO PASSION, BEING TOGETHER WITH A "FRIENDLY" LOVE FOR EACH OTHER IS WHAT FAMILY IS ALL ABOUT!!

NORMALLY, YES.
BUT, THIS WAY WE CAN HAVE THE PASSIONATE LOVE, AND STILL KEEP OUR FAMILY CLOSE TOGETHER.
WE'RE BOTH DOING IT, SO IT'S NOT LIKE WE'RE HAVING AN AFFAIR.
RUSTLE RUSTLE
HAVE YOU GONE INSANE?
COME TO YOUR SENSES!!
MIKI, DARLING...
AFTER MEETING THE MATSUURAS, YOUR FATHER AND I FELT MORE IN LOVE THAN WE HAD IN YEARS...
JUST NOT WITH EACH OTHER.
SO, CAN YOU FORGIVE US?
CRUSH
WHO COULD...
...FORGIVE THEM?!

HUFF
HUFF
HUFF
Wow, Miki, you're really strong.
clap clap clap
I KNOW MY PARENTS HAVE ALWAYS BEEN A BIT STRANGE, BUT THIS TIME...
THEY'VE GONE TOO FAR! I'LL NEVER FORGIVE THEM!!
YOUR PARENTS ARE FUNKY AND COOL. I STILL LIKE THEM.
MEIKO...
That's easy for you to say.
I'M SERIOUS!
THEY'RE MUCH COOLER THAN MY PARENTS.
MY PARENTS...
THANK YOU FOR READING
Marmalade Boy
I'm Miki. Pleased to meet you.
I received lots of letters saying that the girls' uniforms look cute. Don't the boys look sharp too, in their double-breasted suits without ties?
-Wataru Yoshizumi.

...IT'S A MOCKERY OF LOVE. MOM AND DAD ARE BOTH HAVING AFFAIRS, BUT THEY REFUSE TO GET DIVORCED.
MOM THINKS ABOUT HER FINANCES. AND DAD'S JUST CONCERNED WITH APPEARANCES.
WHAT ABOUT **ME**?!
DON'T THEY UNDERSTAND OW DAMAGING IT IS TO WATCH YOUR PARENTS IN UCH A HOLLOW, SPITEFUL MARRIAGE?
I'M...
I'M **NEVER** GETTING MARRIED.
MEIKO...
IS THAT WHY YOU NEVER GO OUT ON DATES?
Even though you're popular.
GLEAM
OH, NO! DON'T GET ME WRONG. I JUST HAVEN'T MET ANYONE WHO'S MY **TYPE**.
I STILL LIKE BOYS. I JUST DON'T WANT TO **MARRY** THEM.
UH-OH.
I'VE GOTTA GO.
WHAT'S GOING ON?
MY FAMILY'S HAVING DINNER WITH THE MATSUURAS.
HAVE TO ALK THE OUR OF HEM OUT OF THIS ONSENSE, NO MATTER WHAT!

GOOD LUCK.
THANKS, MEIKO.
BYE BYE!
GOING HOME?
AREN'T YOU GOING TO GO TO THE TENNIS CLUB MEETING?
GINTA.
I CAN'T COME TODAY. I'VE GOT A FAMILY EMERGENCY.
CAN YOU EXPLAIN THAT TO THE COACH?
FAMILY EMERGENCY?
DID SOMETHING HAPPEN?
WELL,
SORT OF...
BUT, I'VE GOTTA RUN.
I'LL TELL YOU LATER. BYE!
MY PARENTS MAY BE WEIRD,
BUT THEY'RE STILL MY PARENTS.

GRILL, RESTAU
MIKAW
I CAN'T LET THEM DO SOMETHING THIS RIDICULOUS!
I HAVE TO STOP THEM!!
THIS IS OUR DAUGHTER, MIKI.
MIKI,
MEET YOUJI MATSUURA AND HIS WIFE,
CHIYAKO.
PLEASED TO MEET YOU.
IT'S SO NICE TO FINALLY MEET YOU, MIKI.
UH... NICE TO MEET YOU, TOO.
THEY LOOK SO NICE AND... NORMAL.
SO, YOU GUYS ARE GOING TO GET DIVORCED AND SWAP PARTNERS WITH MY PARENTS?
THAT'S RIGHT!
SMILE
THEY ARE NOT NOR-MAL.

# FREE TALK ①

How are you enjoying Marmalade Boy? Are you getting used to reading a story from right to left? In Japan, all books are printed this way! This is the first book from TOKYOPOP® that's printed in the original format.

Traditionally, when manga is brought to America, the artwork is "flipped," so that right-handed people become lefties, and people drive on the wrong side of the road! The artwork you're seeing now is exactly the same as when it was originally printed. Do you think that TOKYOPOP® should print more books this way? Send us your thoughts!

EDITOR
TOKYOPOP®
5900 WILSHIRE BLVD.
SUITE 2000
LOS ANGELES, CA
90036

EDITOR@TOKYOPOP.COM
WWW.TOKYOPOP.COM

SORRY!
AM I LATE?
tha-thump
WHO'S THAT?
HE'S SO... CUTE!
WE JUST STARTED.
THAT'S
OOD.
IS THAT YUU?

YUU,
MEET JIN AND RUMI KOISHIKAWA.
AND THEIR DAUGHTER, MIKI.
daze
smile
HELLO.
OOH!
HE'S SO CUTE WHEN HE SMILES!!
WHAT SHOULD I DO? HE'S MY AGE AND HE'S SOOO CUTE, MAYBE HE WOULD...

WHAT AM I THINKING?!
THERE'S NO TIME FOR THAT!
?
swing swing
OKAY.
WHAT I HAVE TO DO NOW IS...
...
I'M GOING TO GO AHEAD AND SAY IT...
YOU CAN'T DO THIS.
THIS IS JUST INSANE!!
OUR RELATIVES WILL NEVER APPROVE.
OH, DON'T WORRY ABOUT THAT.
I EXPECTED SOME OPPOSITION, BUT WHEN I EXPLAINED THAT THIS IS WHAT YOUR MOTHER AND I WANTED, THEY ALL SUPPORTED OUR DECISION.
MY FAMILY WAS THE SAME WAY.
shake shake
WHAT ABOUT OUR REPUTATION? PEOPLE WILL TALK...
WHAT'S IMPORTANT ARE OUR FEELINGS, RIGHT?
SOMETIMES YOU CAN BE SO HARDHEADED, MIKI.

WHAT ABOUT MY FEELINGS? WHAT ABOUT YUU'S?!
SLAM
HOW DO YOU THINK WE FEEL BEING SHUFFLED AROUND BECAUSE OF YOUR SELFISH GAMES?!
I DON'T CARE.
WHAT?!
...AND YOU DON'T CARE?!
YOUR PARENTS HAVE GONE COMPLETELY MAD...
IF IT MAKES THEM HAPPY, IT'S OKAY BY ME.
YOU SHOULD EAT YOUR SOUP BEFORE IT GETS COLD.

THIS GUY IS WEIRD!
OUR FAMILIES ARE FALLING APART AND HE JUST SITS THERE SIPPING SOUP?
HOW CAN HE BE SO CALM?!
MIKI, DEAR, IT SOUNDS LIKE YOU'RE THE ONLY ONE OPPOSED TO THIS.
IT'S OKAY, HONEY. SHE JUST MET THE MATSUURAS.
MIKI, I'M SURE THAT WHEN YOU GET TO KNOW THE MATSUURAS, YOU'LL SEE WHAT WONDERFUL PEOPLE THEY ARE.
YOU'LL SEE THEM AS FAMILY IN NO TI--
HUH?
Sniff sniff

IF MOM AND DAD DIVORCE AND MARRY DIFFERENT PEOPLE,
THEN WHAT'S GOING TO HAPPEN TO ME?
WHO WOULD I LIVE WITH?
I KNOW THEY HAVEN'T ALWAYS BEEN THE BEST PARENTS.
THEY DON'T SEEM TO CARE HOW I DO ON MY HOMEWORK...
MOM'S A LOUSY COOK,
AND SHE ALWAYS SLEEPS IN LATE...
STAB
STAB
STAB
EVEN THOUGH DAD DOESN'T MAKE MUCH MONEY,
IT DOESN'T STOP HIM FROM SPENDING TOO MUCH ON THINGS HE DOESN'T NEED.
BUT,
THEY ARE STILL MY MOM AND DAD!
I DON'T WANT TO BE SEPARATED
FROM EITHER OF THEM!!!

Silence
TEARS
TEARS
sniff
WE'RE FLATTERED YOU CARE SO MUCH ABOUT US,
BUT THERE'S REALLY NOTHING TO WORRY ABOUT.
THANKS, MIKI, FOR LETTING US KNOW HOW YOU FEEL.
I'm not that bad, am I?
YOU SEE...
WE'RE GOING TO RENT ONE BIG HOUSE AND THE SIX OF US WILL ALL LIVE TOGETHER!
Ack! Grown-ups shouldn't strike a pose!

OUR FAMILY MAKEUP WILL CHANGE, BUT OUR RELATIONSHIPS WON'T.
YOUR FATHER AND I WILL STILL BE YOUR PARENTS.
AND YOU BOTH CAN KEEP YOUR FATHERS' FAMILY NAMES, SO THERE WON'T BE ANY LEGAL CONFUSION.
NOT A BAD IDEA, IS IT?
I told you, don't strike poses!
NO!
SHOCK
YOU'VE GOT TO BE JOKING!
THIS CAN'T BE HAPPENING TO ME!
SO BASICALLY, YOU GUYS ARE ALL GETTING DIVORCED, BUT YOU'RE STILL GOING TO LIVE IN THE SAME HOUSE?
THAT PRETTY MUCH SUMS IT UP.
N-NO...
I CAN'T TAKE THIS...
DIZ
DIZ
WHAT'S WRONG, MIKI?
EVEN AFTER ALL WE SAID, YOU STILL CAN'T SUPPORT US?

NO WAY!
OF COURSE I CAN'T SUPPORT THIS... THIS... THI...
huh?
WHY?
WHY... WHY...
SIGH
WHY IS EVERYBODY LOOKING AT ME LIKE THAT...?!
IT'S MAKING ME LOOK LIKE THE BAD ONE HERE.

WHY DON'T YOU GIVE UP.
F...
SLIP
FINE...
I CAN'T BELIEVE IT!
WHY DOES STUFF LIKE THIS ALWAYS HAPPEN TO ME?!

STILL...
I JUST DON'T GET IT.
kick
YOU'RE IN THE WAY.
......
THEY REALLY DID IT.
DON'T JUST STAND AROUND MOPING.
GRAB A BOX AND GIVE US A HAND!!
MY PARENTS AND THE MATSUURAS REALLY GOT DIVORCED.
AND NOW WE'RE ALL MOVING IN TOGETHER.
We're lucky we found such a nice place!
I know.

THEY CAN'T REMARRY JUST YET.
THE LAW SAYS THEY HAVE TO WAIT SIX MONTHS.
Only women have to wait-men can remarry right away!
SO STARTING TODAY, FOUR COMPLETE STRANGERS AND TWO OF THEIR KIDS ARE SHARING ONE HOUSE... AT LEAST, THAT'S WHAT WE LOOK LIKE IN THE EYES OF THE LAW.
THIS IS INSANE!
CHIYAKO ...
SHOULD I PUT THE CUPBOARD HERE, OR MOVE IT OVER THERE BY THE CORNER?
HMM... I DON'T KNOW...
AND JIN! YOU TOO, YOUJI! WE NEED TO ASK YOUR OPINION.
Miki
Phew
Miki

MIKI!
GET UP.
WE NEED TO GO GET GROCERIES.
The nerve! Who does he think he is?
YOU'RE VERY QUIET TODAY.
WHAT'S THE MATTER? GIVE UP THE FIGHT ALREADY?
AFTER THAT DINNER, I THOUGHT YOU'D NEVER GIVE IN.
SUCH UGLY WORDS DON'T MATCH YOUR PRETTY FACE.
AT LEAST I'VE GOT A PRETTY FACE. YOUR WORDS AND YOUR FACE ARE BOTH UGLY.

I GIVE UP.
MY FAMILY HAS ALWAYS BEEN WEIRD. I SHOULD BE USED TO IT BY NOW.
BESIDES...
THE FOUR OF THEM LOOK SO HAPPY TOGETHER... LIKE THEY'VE BEEN FRIENDS ALL THEIR LIVES.
I CAN'T HELP BUT THINK THAT MAYBE THIS IS BEST FOR THEM.
BUT...
THIS IS JUST TOO WEIRD!
I'M NOT GOING TO FIGHT IT ANY-MORE...
...BUT I'M NEVER GONNA BE COMFORTABLE WITH IT!!

LOOK AT THE BRIGHT SIDE.
NOW YOU'LL HAVE TWICE AS MANY FAMILY MEMBERS!
DON'T HATE IT SO MUCH.
LET'S JUST BE FRIENDS,
OKAY?!
shake♡
BLUSH
OH... I GUESS HE'S COOL AFTER ALL.
WELL...
OKAY.
GRASP
?
HE GAVE ME SOME-THING.

His wad of gum
YUU!!
AH HA HA HA HA HA!
WHY THAT LITTLE...!!
MAKING FUN OF ME...

AAAARGH!!
WAIT A MINUTE, YUU!
DID YOU DO ANYTHING TO MIKI? SHE SEEMS VERY UPSET AGAIN.
HA, HA!
IT'S JUST SO MUCH FUN TO PLAY JOKES ON HER.
Go easy on her.
........
YUU...
YOU'VE BEEN TAKING ALL OF THIS CHANGE VERY WELL.
YOU HAVEN'T COMPLAINED TO YOUR FATHER OR ME.
BUT ARE YOU **SURE** YOU'RE FINE WITH ALL OF THIS?
YOU DON'T HAVE ANY OBJECTIONS?
REALLY, MOM, IT'S OKAY.
IF YOU AND DAD ARE HAPPY, THEN IT'S FINE BY ME.
YUU...

HOW'S IT GOING, MIKI? ALL SQUARED AWAY?
YUP.
MIKI...
NOW, I WANT YOU TO BE NICE TO THE MAT-SUURAS.
I KNOW.
YUU, TOO.
I KNOW.
BUT,
DON'T FALL IN LOVE WITH HIM.
HUH?
I SAID, DON'T FALL IN LOVE WITH YUU.

OUR NEW HOUSEHOLD IS COMPLICATED ENOUGH AS IT IS. IF YOU AND HE WERE TO FALL IN LOVE, THINGS WOULD BE EVEN CRAZIER AROUND HERE.
And whose fault do you think that is?
SO TRUE...
OKAY? JUST REMEMBER, WE'RE ALL FAMILY NOW.
YEAH, YEAH.
I GET IT, AL- READY.
WELL, LET'S GO DOWN- STAIRS THEN.
OKAY.
WHAT'S MOM WORRIED ABOUT?
WOW!
EVERY- THING LOOKS SO GOOD.
I ADMIT, HE'S REALLY CUTE (I'VE CAUGHT MYSELF FALLING UNDER HIS SPELL ON SEVERAL OCCASIONS).

CHEERS ☆
BUT,
ANYONE WHO COULD SO CALMLY GO ALONG WITH ALL THIS CRAZINESS...
I'LL **NEVER** FALL IN LOVE WITH HIM!

MEIKO! GOOD MORNING.
HEY, MIKI.
FINISHED MOVING YET?
YEAH, I GUESS.
NOW MY CRAZY NEW LIFE CAN BEGIN.
YOU SEEM PRETTY CHEERFUL NOW.
THAT'S BE-CAUSE I'M GOING TO SCHOOL!
IF I'M AT SCHOOL, I DON'T HAVE TO BE AROUND THAT CRAZY FAMILY.
SCHOOL IS THE ONLY PLACE WHERE I CAN GET SOME...
WACK
...PEACE.
HEY!
WHO DID THAT?

Y-
YUU?!
WHA-WHAT ARE YOU DOING HERE?
WHY ARE YOU WEARING OUR UNIFORM?
IT'S A PAIN HAVING TO WALK ALL THE WAY TO YOKOHAMA,
SO I TRANSFERRED HERE.
RUMI SUGGESTED IT TO ME. SHE SAID THAT THIS SCHOOL OFFERS A LOT OF FREEDOM TO ITS STUDENTS, AND IT EVEN HAS AN ESCALATOR PROGRAM*!
NOBODY TOLD ME ANYTHING ABOUT A TRANSFER.
IF WE HAD TOLD YOU, YOU'D JUST HAVE MADE A **FUSS**. IT'S EASIER JUST LEAVING YOU IN THE DARK.

*MIKI'S HIGH SCHOOL OFFERS ITS STUDENTS EASY ACCEPTANCE TO THE LOCAL UNIVERSITY. SCHOOLS WITH ESCALATOR PROGRAMS ARE PRESTIGIOUS AND EXPENSIVE.

NOW YOU HAVE TO PUT UP WITH YOUR **CRAZY** FAMILY AT SCHOOL, TOO.
HEH HEH
SUCKS TO BE YOU.
......!!
He was spying on me!
NOW, SHOW ME WHERE THE MAIN OFFICE IS.
TODAY'S MY FIRST DAY, SO I'LL NEED YOU TO SHOW ME AROUND...
WHAT A NIGHT-MARE.
drag drag
MEIKO, WHO'S THAT? A TRANSFER STUDENT?
OH, HI, GINTA.
LOOKS LIKE IT.
Yokohama's not so far. Why don't you just commute?
This was my school first!
A FRIEND OF MIKI'S?

HE'S KIND-OF LIKE A BROTHER, I GUESS.
KIND OF...?
What's that supposed to mean?
........
DID YOU HEAR?! THERE'S A NEW TRANSFER STUDENT IN 1-B!
A BOY!
YEAH? SO WHAT.
I HEAR HE'S REALLY HOT!!

FIRST DAY HERE AND HE'S ALREADY MR. POPULAR.
WELL, IT'S NO SURPRISE WITH HIS GOOD LOOKS.
WHY DID HE HAVE TO END UP IN MY CLASS...?
DO YOU MIND IF I CALL YOU YUU?
WE'RE ALL GOOD FRIENDS HERE, SO WE MOSTLY GO BY OUR FIRST NAMES.
SURE.
THEN IS IT ALRIGHT IF I CALL YOU BY YOUR FIRST NAMES, TOO?
Oh, yes! Yes!
I'm Atsuko!
I'm Mie!
HMPH.
MIKI!
THERE'S AN OPEN COURT. WANNA COME PRACTICE WITH ME?
UH, SURE!

MAT-
SUURA.
WACK
WACK
WACK

YOU WERE WALKING WITH MIKI THIS MORNING...
MEIKO AKI-ZUKI.
PLEASED TO MEET YOU.
IF YOU'RE LOOKING FOR MIKI, SHE'S OVER THERE.
THAT BOY, HE'S IN OUR CLASS, RIGHT?
YEAH,
HIS NAME IS GINTA SUOU.
MIKI'S BOY-FRIEND?
NO,
BUT THEY'RE REALLY CLOSE.
THEY'VE BEEN GOOD FRIENDS SINCE JUNIOR HIGH.
SO, IS SUOU GOING TO ASK HER OUT, OR WHAT?
......
THAT'S NOT GOING TO HAPPEN.

POOR MIKI.
A FEW YEARS BACK, SHE TOLD HIM THAT SHE LOVED HIM,
BUT HE... DIDN'T FEEL THE SAME WAY.
OH...

HELLO, TORYO HIGH!
THIS IS THE BROADCAST CLUB, COMING TO YOU LIVE WITH THE LUNCHTIME NEWS.
WE'VE GOT A SPECIAL GUEST IN THE STUDIO TODAY.
HE'S THE HOT TRANSFER STUDENT IN CLASS 1-B THAT ALL THE GIRLS ARE TALKING ABOUT...
SAY HELLO TO YUU MATSUURA!
THANK YOU,
IT'S A PLEASURE TO BE HERE.
CHEER
......
THAT IDIOT.

WOW YOUR STEP-BROTHER LOOKS REALLY GOOD ON TELEVISION, TOO.
IGNORE... IGNORE... IGNORE. I'M NOT LISTENING! WHY SHOULD I CARE WHAT HE SAYS ON TV?
YOU'RE AN ATHLETE, AN HONOR STUDENT, AND FROM WHAT I'VE HEARD, YOU'RE QUITE POPULAR WITH THE LADIES. SPEAKING OF LADIES...
...A LOT O THE GIRLS ARE WONDERIN IF YOU'RE ELIGIBLE,
BUT YOU'VE BEEN SEEN WALKING TO SCHOOL WITH A CERTAIN GIRL.
STUDIO
OH, YOU MEAN MIKI...?
YES! MIKI KOISHIKAWA, ALSO IN CLASS 1-B. YOU TWO SEEM AWFULLY CLOSE.
HOW EXACTLY DO YOU KNOW EACH OTHER?

miki

WE'RE LIVING TOGETHER.
CALM
WOW!! WHAT A SURPRISE!
YOU HEARD IT HERE FIRST!
rustle
SO, THE TWO OF YOU ARE SHACKING UP...
WELL, NOT EXACTLY...
JUST HOLD ON A SECOND!
SLAM!
LET ME EXPLAIN THIS.
HUFF
HUFF
HUFF
MY PARENTS AND HIS PARENTS ARE JUST GOOD FRIENDS,
HUFF
SO OUR FAMILIES HAVE BEEN LIVING TOGETHER IN ONE HOUSE. THAT'S ALL! THERE'S NOTHING GOING ON!
HUFF
AH... OKAY...

whispe
AREN'T YOU TWISTING THE FACTS A BIT?
I DON'T CARE!!
IF THE TRUTH GETS OUT, I'LL BE THE LAUGHING-STOCK OF THE SCHOOL!
AS YOU JUST HEARD, IT' NOT JUST MIKI AND YUU THAT ARE SHACKING UP,
BUT THEIR PARENTS, AS WELL!
I JUST SAID WE HAVE THE SAME ADDRESS.
DON'T CHANGE THE STORY!
YOU GUYS ARE ALWAYS BLOWING THINGS OUT OF PROPORTIO
AND WHAT'S WITH USING MY PICTURE?!
WA
WAAA, I'M SORRY, I'M SORRY!
WA
CAN I GO NOW?
I HAVEN'T HAD LUNCH YET.
SORRY, JUST ONE MORE MINUTE...
GYA GYA
aha ha ha ha
DID YOU SEE THE LOOK ON HIS FACE?!
ha ha ha
THEY'RE REALLY SCARED OF MIKI.

HMPH.
HOW ABSURD.
YOU IDIOT!
THANKS TO YOU AND THE ROADCAST CLUB, EVERYONE LAUGHED AT ME.
DON'T BLAME ME.
YOU'RE THE ONE WHO BURST IN AND MADE A SCENE.
I'm the one who should be embarrassed!
OH, YEAH?
WELL, IF I HADN'T GONE ON, YOU WOULD HAVE TOLD EVERYBODY ABOUT UR FAMILY.
Who cares?
I do!
KOISHI-KAWA,
AT-UURA!

I SAW THE BROAD-CAST.
IT SURE WAS WILD.
NACHAN!
IT WAS VERY AMUSING. YOU TWO WILL HAVE TO GO ON AGAIN.
PLEASE, NO.
NACHAN.
YOU'RE MY HOMEROOM TEACHER, YOU'VE BEEN TO MY HOUSE, YOU KNOW MY SITUATION...
PLEASE, DON'T TELL ANYONE ABOUT MY FAMILY!!
O-OKAY...
I GOT-CHA.
I KNOW THIS MUST BE DIFFICULT FOR YOU TWO,
BUT I THINK YOU CAN HANDLE IT.
OKAY!
THANK YOU.

ISN'T THAT MR. NAMURA?
WHY DO YOU CALL HIM NACHAN?
JUST BE-CAUSE...
HE'S REALLY NICE AND VERY POPULAR.
BECAUSE HE'S SO YOUNG, HE LETS US CALL HIM NACHAN.
HE'S THE ADVISOR FOR MY TENNIS CLUB, TOO.
BY THE WAY, WHICH CLUB ARE YOU GOING TO JOIN?
WELL,
I WAS IN THE TENNIS CLUB IN JUNIOR HIGH, BUT--
WHAT?! GIVE IT UP!
YOU'RE NOT JOINING MY CLUB.
THAT'S OKAY.
I DIDN'T WANT TO JOIN YOUR STUPID CLUB, ANYWAY.
I DON'T PLAN ON JOINING ANY CLUBS.
I DIDN'T JOIN ANY AT MY PREVIOUS SCHOOL, EITHER.
OH...
WHY NOT?
I'VE GOT A LOT OF THINGS I NEED TO DO,
AND I CAN'T HAVE EXTRA-CURRICULAR ACTIVITIES EATING UP MY TIME.

## FREE TALK ②

I got the name Miki from a model named Miki Yoshida that used to be in the magazine *MC Sister.* She was the poster girl and was often on the cover. I also liked her name, so I thought about using that name someday in one of my stories. I used the name Mio before, so I received letters from the readers asking if I liked names beginning with "Mi".♪ (I wrote one with a Miyoko as well.) It wasn't on purpose! For the heroine of my next story, I'll make sure that her name doesn't start with "Mi."♪

- Wataru Yoshizumi

A JOB...? STUDYING?
......
SOME-THING LIKE THAT.
HMMM...
IF HE'S PLANNING ON GOING TO OUR LOCAL COLLEGE, HE DOESN'T NEED TO WORRY ABOUT HIS EXAM SCORES.
MAYBE HE'S PLANNING ON GOING SOME-WHERE ELSE.
THAT'S A LONG WAYS OFF. I'LL WORRY ABOUT THAT LATER...
HEY,
WHAT'S THAT BUILDING OVER THERE?
WHAT? OH, THAT.
THAT'S THE OLD PUBLIC LIBRARY.

HUH?
WE HAVE A PUBLIC LIBRARY IN THE SCHOOL?
No wonder I couldn't find the school library.
THAT PLACE IS FULL OF BORING OLD BOOKS, SO NO ONE USES IT.
MEIKO GOES THERE ONCE IN A WHILE, BUT THEN, SHE'S IN THE LITERARY CLUB.
YOU HAVEN'T EATEN LUNCH YET, HAVE YOU?
BELL'S ABOUT TO RING. YOU SHOULD HURRY...
NAH...
I'M CUTTING 5TH PERIOD. I'LL EAT IT THEN.
I'LL SHOW UP FOR 6TH PERIOD P.E.
SEE YA.
WHAT?!
WHAT DO YOU MEAN, "SEE YA"? YUU...?
AHHH!
RING
RING
RING
RING
RING

NOT BAD.
I LIKE THIS PLACE.

WHISTLE
dribble
dribble
dribble
search
search
THERE HE IS.
HE ACTUALLY CAME BACK.
WHAT IS HE UP TO?
I JUST DON'T GET HIS BEHAVIOR...
MIKI!
MIKI!
MM?
WHY DIDN'T YOU TELL US YOU WERE LIVING WITH YUU?
I MEAN, I COULD TELL THE TWO OF YOU KNEW EACH OTHER, BUT THIS...!
OH,
IT'S NO BIG DEAL.
OUR PARENTS ARE FRIENDS, BUT IT DOESN'T AFFECT US.
ARE YOU CRAZY?!
WHAT I WOULDN'T GIVE TO BE IN YOUR SHOES!

WEIRD?
THE GUY'S ALL LOOKS!
HIS PERSONALITY IS JUST... WEIRD!
WELL, IT'S HARD TO EXPLAIN.
Can't really give an example.
HE'S VERY SWEET...
...AND KIND, TOO.
THAT JERK.
HE'S ALWAYS MAKING FUN OF ME, BUT HE ACTS ALL NICE IN FRONT OF THE OTHER GIRLS.
Yesterday he helped me hand out flyers, and today he...
WAAA
GO, MATSUURA!

OH?
HE'S PRETTY GOOD AT SPORTS.
I WONDER IF HE'S GOOD AT TENNIS...
WHAT A SHOW-OFF!

What's Ginta doing here?
Came to pick up the ball.
I BET HE'S JUST A JOCK. HIS GRADES MUST BE LOUSY.
I DOUBT IT. OUR ENTRANCE EXAMS ARE PRETTY TOUGH, SO HE MUST HAVE HAD GOOD GRADES.
......
STOMP STOMP STOMP
What his deal?
DO YOU THINK YUU'S SO PERFECT THAT OTHER GUYS ARE INTIMIDATED?
NOT ALL GUYS.
JUST GINTA.
HE'S AFRAID THAT YUU MIGHT TAKE MIKI.

NO...
THAT CAN'T BE.
I WAS REJECTED BY GINTA A LONG TIME AGO.
OH?
REALLY?
I'M SORRY, I DIDN'T KNOW.
WHISTLE
GROUP 2, YOU'RE UP!
Stupid, every-one knows.
Well, they seem so close.
MIKI...
I FORGOT TO TELL YOU, BUT... I WAS TALKING TO YUU,
AND I KIND OF TOLD HIM THE WHOLE STORY ABOUT YOU AND GINTA.
MM?
I WAS CAUGHT UP IN THE MOMENT.
WAS THAT WRONG OF ME?
NO PROBLEM. THAT HAPPENED AGES AGO!
IT DOESN'T BOTHER ME.
I'M SORRY...
NO, REALLY. DON'T WORRY.

OH, GINTA...
THERE WAS A TIME WHEN JUST LOOKING AT YOU MADE MY HEART POUND.
THAT WASN'T SO LONG AGO...
NOW WE'RE JUST FRIENDS.
BUT, BACK THEN I WAS ALWAYS THINKING ABOUT GINTA.
AT SCHOOL I NEVER TOOK MY EYES OFF OF HIM.
WHEN I GOT HOME, I'D THINK ABOUT THE CONVERSATIONS WE'D HAD THAT DAY.
I REALLY, REALLY LOVED HIM.
...

TWO YEARS AGO
MIKI!
ID YOU SEE THE MATCH ESTER-DAY?
THE TAPAN OPEN INALS VERE ON TV!
I SAW IT.
STEFAN EDBERG WAS AWESOME!
I WISH I HAD HIS BACKHAND.
THEY LOOK SO CUTE TOGETHER.
THEY'RE NOT GOING OUT, ARE THEY?
Don't you think my serve looks like Edberg's?
Huh? You wish!
NOT YET.
UT IT'S ONLY A ATTER TIME...

# FREE TALK ③

Miki and Yuu are first year students, so you might think that they are Freshmen--that's not really the case! In Japan, middle school and high school are each three years long, instead of two years and four years respectively, as they typically are in America. So you see, Miki and Yuu are really more like Sophomores!

Another difference between Japanese schools and some American ones is the taking of entrance exams to get into high school. Students take tests in Japanese, Math, Social Studies, Science, and English, although private schools may have other tests as well. Choosing the right high school is important, as certain high schools are better than others for transferring to certain universities, so competition can be quite fierce.

Oh, one more thing -- in Japan, high school is optional! Students are only required to go to school through junior high, but that doesn't stop more than 75% of young adults from attending high school.

- Editor

WHAT?!
I CAN'T DO THAT!
I DON'T SEE WHY NOT. IT'LL BE OKAY.
OU GUYS RE SUCH GOOD FRIENDS, ANYWAY.
WELL...
I KNOW HE DOESN'T HATE ME.
SEE? NOTHIN' TO WORRY ABOUT.
DO IT, DO IT!
That's easy for you to say, Meiko!
WHAT IF HE DOESN'T FEEL THE SAME WAY
ABOUT ME AS I DO ABOUT HIM?
I DON'T HAVE THE COURAGE TO TELL HIM.
I'M AFRAID TO KNOW THE TRUTH.

CAAW
MAAW
WHAT'S THIS?
IT'S A PIN FROM WIMBLEDON. MY COUSIN BROUGHT ME BACK TWO OF THEM FROM HIS TRIP TO LONDON,
SO, I THOUGHT I'D GIVE YOU ONE.
ARE YOU SURE...?!
DON'T TELL ANYONE I GAVE THIS TO YOU.
WE'LL EACH HAVE ONE, OKAY?
Put it away!
O-OKAY.
THANK YOU!
Don't lose it.
GINTA...

HE'S GOT A LOT OF OTHER FRIENDS IN THE TENNIS CLUB HE COULD HAVE GIVEN IT TO.
BUT HE CHOSE TO GIVE IT TO ME?
ONLY TO ME...?
GINTA...
CAN THIS MEAN...
...YOU FEEL THE SAME WAY I DO?
WHAT?
YOU GAVE HIM A LOVE LETTER?!

MEIKO, NOT SO LOUD!
HUSH HUSH
There's no one here.
I SEE... NO WONDER YOU'VE BEEN ACTING FUNNY TODAY.
I WONDER WHAT HE THOUGHT...
I'm a lousy writer.
DON'T WORRY! I'M SURE HE'LL BE DELIGHTED!
I'M SO PROUD OF YOU, MIKI.
GOOD JOB!
AH!!! OH, NO!
I LEFT MY GYM CLOTHES AT SCHOOL!
I'VE GOTTA GO BACK FOR THEM.
GO ON HOME WITHOUT ME.
It's because you were only thinking about Ginta.
Bleh

2-E
DEAR GINTA, EVER SINCE WE ENTERED JUNIOR HIGH, I'VE REALLY LIKED YOU.
ha ha ha ha
SHE'S GOT A CRUSH ON YOU! WHAT'RE YOU GONNA DO?
YOU DON'T ACTUALLY LIKE HER, DO YOU, GINTA?
WELL,
WE GET ALONG REALLY WELL AND WE TALK A LOT...
WE'RE JUST GOOD FRIENDS. NOTHING MORE.
GETTING A LETTER LIKE THIS DOESN'T CHA--
lick

RATTLE
MI-
MIKI!
I'M SORRY! I...

MIKI!!

HONK
HONK
HONK
DRIP
DRIP
DRIP

JUST FRIENDS.
WELL, THAT'S OKAY.
BUT...
YOU DIDN'T HAVE TO SHOW IT TO THOSE GUYS!
HOW DID I EVER FALL FOR YOU?!
GINTA, YOU'RE A JERK!!

HEY, MIKI?
YOU HAVEN'T CHANGED YOUR HAIR-STYLE.
WHAT ARE YOU TALKING ABOUT?
WHEN YOUR HEART IS BROKEN, IT'S TRADITIONAL TO CUT YOUR HAIR.
OKAY...
WHAT ARE YOU SMILING ABOUT?
BECAUSE I'M HAPPY! NOW I DON'T HAVE TO WORRY ABOUT THAT GINTA TAKING AWAY MY MIKI!
HEY!
I'M JUST TRYING TO EASE YOUR PAIN.
Trying to be cheerful...
MEIKO...
I'D RATHER YOU FOUND ANOTHER WAY TO COMFORT ME.
I THOUGHT YOU'D SKIP SCHOOL TODAY.
I DIDN'T WANT TO COME,
BUT I CAN'T JUST STAY HOME WHENEVER I'M FEELING DOWN, SO I DRAGGED MYSELF HERE ANYWAY.
HAHAHA
SOUNDS LIKE YOU.

WHY DON'T YOU CUT YOUR HAIR ANYWAY, JUST FOR FUN?
ARE YOU KIDDING?!
IF IT WAS ANY SHORTER I'D BE BALD AS A MONK!
RUSTLE

pu
WAHAHAHAHA!
EXPLODE
WHAT HAPPENED TO YOUR HAIR, GINTA?!
YOU LOOK LIKE A MONKEY!
AHAHAHAHAHA
HA...
CLICK
whisper whisper
What's this?
What happened to Ginta?
HE CUT HIS HAIR...
I WONDER IF THAT'S HIS WAY OF
APOLO-GIZING?

BEEP
AH, MEMORIES.
IT SEEMS LIKE SO LONG AGO.
SIGH
She daydreamed while playing.
THAT DAY, GINTA LOOKED A LOT SADDER THAN I DID.
FOR THE NEXT YEAR AND A HALF, GINTA AND I DIDN'T SAY A WORD TO EACH OTHER.
THEN ONE DAY, HE CAME UP TO ME AS IF NOTHING HAD HAPPENED.
Hey, Miki! We're going to be in the same class next year,
Class B.
Meiko, too.
EVEN THOUGH I WAS THINKING, "WHAT'S UP WITH HIM?" I RESPONDED AS IF NOTHING HAD HAPPENED...
Really? They've already announced the classes for next year?
I should go check the bulletin board.
AND AFTER THAT, WE STARTED TALKING TO EACH OTHER MORE AND MORE.
I GUESS THINGS ARE EXACTLY LIKE THEY WERE BEFORE.

WELL, NOT "EXACTLY." I DON'T HAVE A CRUSH ON HIM LIKE I DID THEN.
WE'RE FRIENDS AGAIN, AND THAT'S A GOOD THING, BUT I CAN'T HELP BUT WONDER IF--
HEY, MIKI!
WATCH OUT!!
HUH?
WHAM
KYAHHHHHH
MIKI!!

Nurse's Office
HOW DO YOU FEEL?
MMM.
MUCH BETTER...
I'LL BRING YOUR BAG AND CLOTHES, OKAY?
OKAY.
THANKS.
RATTLE RATTLE
IT'S MY FAULT FOR DAYDREAMING LIKE THAT.
HOW STUPID OF ME.

OH, MATSUURA.
ARGH! YUU?!
OH, NO! HE'S GOING TO MAKE FUN OF ME AGAIN.
panic
panic
HOW'S MIKI DOING?
SHE'S SEEMS TO BE JUST FINE.
I'M GOING TO GET HER UNIFORM NOW.
You klutz.
What a disgrace.
Nowhere to hide...
MIKI.
I KNOW!
I'LL JUST PRETEND TO BE ASLEEP.
EVEN HE WOULDN'T DISTURB A SLEEPING PATIENT.
Oh wait, he might...!
Wake up!
SHE'S ASLEEP?

ARE YOU SLEEPING,
MIKI?

.......
shya
rattle rattle
shut

WAKE!
blush
WHA...?
WHA
WHA
WHA
WHAT WAS THAT ALL ABOUT?!

WELL, I'M OFF TO WORK!
SEE YOU LATER.
stand
WAIT UP, JIN.
I'M GOING, TOO.
Miki
TUG

I NEED TO GO DOWN TO THE DINING ROOM AT SOME POINT...
BUT IF I GO, I'LL RUN INTO YUU.
I SKIPPED DINNER AND HID IN MY ROOM LAST NIGHT TO AVOID HIM.
WHAT DID HE MEAN...
...BY THAT?!
BLUSH
I DON'T KNOW HOW TO ACT WHEN I SEE HIM!
GRRR...

Yuu

WELL, AS FAR AS HE KNOWS, I WAS SNOOZING.
SO, I'LL JUST ACT LIKE NOTHING HAPPENED.
CLICK
GOOD MOR-NING.
ER, G-GOOD MOR-NING.
thump
W-WHERE IS EVERY-BODY?

THEY ALL LEFT FOR WORK.
OH, YEAH... I SEE. WELL, UM... YEAH.
SINCE WE'RE SO CLOSE TO SCHOOL, WE CAN TAKE IT EASY.
By the way...
Jin - Banker
Youji - Businessman
Rumi - Cosmetics maker
Chiyako - Brewer
whoosh
Mainichi Shimbun
.....
stare
WHAT? YOU WANT TO READ THE NEWS-PAPER?
OH, NO. NOT REALLY...

rustle
HERE YOU GO.
YUU, WHY ARE YOU GIVING ME THE CALENDAR SECTION?
THAT'S THE ONLY PART YOU READ, ANYWAY.
WHAT?!
I READ OTHER SECTIONS, TOO!
YOUR HOROSCOPE?
FUNNIES?
YOUR TOAST IS READY.
.....
Can't argue with that.
WHATEVER. COULD YOU PASS ME THE APRICOT JAM?

NONE LEFT.
Ate it all.
ALL WE'VE GOT IS THIS.
OH... MARMA-LADE?
I DON'T LIKE THAT STUFF.
FINE CUT Breakfast Orange MARMALADE
DON'T BE PICKY.
BUT, IT'S SO BITTER. ESPECIALLY THE RINDS.
.....
YOU KNOW, YUU. YOU'RE A LOT LIKE MARMA-LADE.
HUH?
EVEN THOUGH YOU'VE GOT LOTS OF BITTER BITS INSIDE YOU,
ALL PEOPLE SEE IS THE SWEETNESS ON THE SURFACE.
MARMA-LADE BOY!
PERFECT, ISN'T IT?!

HMPH.
I SEE.
What a perfect comparison. ♡
WELL THEN, MIKI, YOU'RE THIS...
ALWAYS SPICY AND SOUR...
A MUSTARD GIRL!
perfect! ♡
FAUCHON
mustard
200g
......!!
BAM
WELL, I'LL BE GOING NOW.
HEY, YUU! GET BACK HERE!
YOU'VE GOTTA HELP ME DO THE DISHES!

WHAT'S HIS PROBLEM?
GRRR... IT'S NOT FAIR!!
HE HASN'T CHANGED A BIT!
SPLOOOOSH
THAT KISS MUST'VE BEEN A FLUKE.
WHY WASTE TIME FREAKING OUT?
I'LL JUST PRETEND IT NEVER HAPPENED!!
KNOCK
KNOCK
MIKI?
...
YES?

click
WHY DON'T YOU JOIN THE GANG DOWN-STAIRS?
YOUR MOTHER AND I MADE CHOCOLATE CAKE.
OH, I'M SORRY. WERE YOU STUDY-ING?
YEAH, I JUST CAN'T FIGURE OUT THIS PROB-LEM...
GEOMETRY, RIGHT? WHY DON'T YOU ASK YOUJI? HE'S GREAT AT MATH. YOU CAN GET A LESSON AND A SNACK, TOO!
REALLY?
I THINK I'LL DO THAT.
voom bam doom zoom
Go left-- I mean right! Just shoot it!
GABOOM
DEAD AGAIN?!
HAHAHAHAHAHA
JIN, YOU REALLY SUCK AT THIS GAME.
...SO YOU CARRY THE THREE, AND THERE'S THE ANSWER!
SEE?
AH! NOW IT MAKES SENSE.
I GET IT! I GET IT!

IS THAT TODAY'S HOMEWORK? I LUCKED OUT! ♡
LET ME COPY IT LATER!
Pikuum zoom...
BAGOOOM
Ah...
REALLY?
HA HA HA HA
YOU'RE A GREAT TEACHER, YOUJI.
YOU MAKE IT SO EASY TO UNDER-STAND!
数学 I
COME JOIN US, YUU. WE CAN ALL DO IT TOGETHER.
NAAA
NO WAY.
AW, COME ON!
HAHAHAHA
Dad's pathetic at video games, isn't he?
Give me another chance!
YOU JUST DON'T HAVE THE SKILLS.
GIVE IT UP, JIN.
GRAB!
WAIT, YUU! DON'T GO!!
YOU HAVE TO SHOW ME HOW TO BEAT THIS GAME!!

HA...
stand
SOMETHING WRONG, MIKI?
UMM... NO.
NOTHING'S WRONG.
I JUST THINK I SHOULD FINISH MY HOMEWORK BY MYSELF. THANKS FOR HELPING ME WITH IT, YOUJI.
CAN I GET YOU ANOTHER CUP OF TEA, MIKI?
N-NO THANKS! I'M FINE!
DASH
AND THANKS FOR THE CAKE!

......
SLAM
NO!
I CAN'T BELIEVE IT!
I'M ACTUALLY GETTING USED TO MY
INSANE FAMILY!!

I PROMISED MYSELF I WOULDN'T GO ALONG WITH THEM...
...BUT I'VE BEEN INFECTED BY THEIR CHEERY GOOD NATURE!
I CAN'T GIVE IN!!
WHY NOT?
WHAT'S WRONG WITH LIVING HAPPILY TOGETHER?
WELL, YOU COULD JUST GO ALONG AND TRY TO ENJOY YOURSELF...
NO!
IT'S NO GOOD!
IF THEY'RE GOING TO LIVE LIKE CRAZY PEOPLE, THEN I WANT TO BE THE NORMAL ONE IN THE FAMILY.
I'LL STOP CRITICIZING WHAT THEY'RE DOING,
BUT I'M CERTAINLY NOT GOING TO PLAY THEIR LITTLE GAME!

MIKI,
YOU FINISHED CLEANING?
UH, NOT QUITE. ALMOST.
I'LL BE WAITING AT THE MAIN ENTRANCE.
OH?
GOING HOME TOGETHER?
NO!
I'M NOT WALKING WITH HIM! DON'T BE STUPID.
IT'S JUST, TODAY IS MOM'S BIRTHDAY, AND I DON'T HAVE MUCH MONEY. YUU SAID WE COULD POOL OUR MONEY AND GET HER SOMETHING NICE TOGETHER.
YOU CAN'T BLAME ME FOR WANTING TO GET MY MOM A COOL GIFT, CAN YOU?!
HMMMM.
THAT'S ALL THERE IS TO IT, I SWEAR!
GRIN GRIN

YOU COMPLAIN ABOUT YOUR FAMILY ALL THE TIME, MIKI...
...BUT THINGS LOOK PRETTY COZY TO ME.
ARE YOU SURE RUMI WILL LIKE THESE?
AGATHA
TRUST ME!
ALL THE COOL YOUNG GIRLS ARE WEARING THOSE EARRINGS!
She likes to dress like a teenager.
I'll tell her you said that.
WE'RE BACK...
Crack

WHAT HAPPENED?
WHAT WAS THAT NOISE?!
dash
dash
M-
MOM...?
IT'S NOTHING. THE VASE BROKE, THAT'S ALL.
YOU TWO, PLEASE GO TO YOUR ROOMS.

LOOKS LIKE THEY HAD A FIGHT.
THE WAY THEY WERE STANDING THERE...
Looks pretty bad.
WELL, I GUESS THE BIRTHDAY PARTY'S OFF.
Man, I'm hungry.
WHAT SHOULD WE DO ABOUT DINNER?
.....
WHY...?
BUT THEY ALWAYS GET ALONG SO WELL.
WHAT HAPPENED?!

I DON'T KNOW THE DETAILS.
SEEMS LIKE MY PARENTS AND YOURS DIDN'T SEE EYE-TO-EYE.
SOMEHOW, IT TURNED INTO A FIGHT.
Jin told me.
I SEE...
I HATE TO ADMIT IT, BUT I MISS THE SUPER HAPPY FAMILY.
I HOPE THEY MAKE UP SOON.
YEAH, I KNOW.

......
JEALOUS?
URK
NO!
IT'S OTHING LIKE THAT!
NOTHING LIKE THAT...

CRACK
uh?
again?
I CAN'T TAKE IT!
I DON'T WANT TO LIVE LIKE THIS ANY MORE!!
SUPERVISION
POLO 1992

YOU'RE RIGHT.
SIXTEEN YEARS OF MARRIAGE IS A LONG TIME.
CHANGING PARTNERS, LIVING IN THE SAME HOUSE... I GUESS IT WAS TOO BIG A CHANGE.
YEAH.
WE'D BE BETTER OFF GOING BACK TO HOW WE WERE BEFORE.
FORGET ABOUT LIVING TOGETHER.
WHAT?!

## FREE TALK ④

I've always been a big tennis fan. In school, I was a member of the tennis team, just like Miki and Ginta. That's why I've made that a main side story (but I regret that I can't focus on it more). With my experience, I'm confident I can write about such things with great realism. I really don't have time to play the game any-more, but I take great pleasure from watching it on TV. I got satellite TV just so I can watch tennis! Hopefully I won't miss the Australian Open this year.

- Wataru Yoshizumi

WE'LL GO BACK TO THE WAY
WE WERE LIVING BEFORE...
...AND NEVER MEET AGAIN.
YEAH.
IT'S FOR THE BEST.
ARGH!
THINGS ARE MOVING TOO FAST. I CAN'T KEEP UP!
PANIC
WHY IS THIS HAPPENING?
SO, AM I TRANS-FERRING
BACK TO MY OLD SCHOOL?
SORRY, YUU,
BUT IT WOULD BE BETTER IF WE BROKE ALL CONTACT WITH THE KOISHIKAWAS.

THAT'S TOO BAD.
Will they even let me switch back?
I WAS JUST GETTING USED TO THIS SCHOOL.
WAIT...
WAIT A SECOND!!
POLO
1992

DON'T YOU THINK YOU'RE CALLING IT QUITS A BIT QUICKLY?!
DIDN'T YOU THINK THROUGH THIS STUFF BEFORE YOU GOT DIVORCED AND REMARRIED?!
WHAT'S WRONG, MIKI?
YOU WERE SO OPPOSED TO THIS ARRANGE- MENT BEFORE.
WE'RE GOING BACK TO HOW OUR FAMILY USED TO BE.
AREN'T YOU HAPPY?
I KNOW THAT'S WHAT I WANTED,
BUT...
BUT?
I STILL
THINK THIS FAMILY IS WEIRD.
BUT, YOU'RE ALL SUCH NICE PEOPLE...
...I WAS STARTING TO BELIEVE
THAT IT MIGHT ACTUALLY WORK OUT.
POLO
1992

## FREE TALK ⑤

*Marmalade Boy* is the most popular story by Wataru Yoshizumi, but it's not her only series. The 39-year-old manga-ka's first book was a romance called *Radical Romance*. She hit the big-time with *Handsome Girlfriend*, the story of a teenage model/actress. (Look for a cameo by the series' star, Mio Hagiwara, in the next chapter of *Marmalade Boy*!) Her latest works include *Mintna Bokura* and *Random Walk*. Her manga first appeared in the magazine anthology *Ribon*, one of the most popular shojo magazines in Japan (*Kodocha** - *Sana's Stage* also first appeared in *Ribon*).
- Editor

* *Kodocha* now available from TOKYOPOP!

REALLY?!
YOU DON'T KNOW HOW HAPPY WE ARE TO HEAR THAT!!
YAY
WHAT?
WHAT?
WHAT?
SORRY TO SCARE YOU.
WE WEREN'T SURE WHETHER OR NOT YOU'D FINALLY ACCEPTED EVERYTHING, SO WE PUT ON THIS PLAY TO FIND OUT.
YOU'VE BEEN STUBBORN ON PURPOSE SO YOU WOULDN'T GET USED TO THINGS, RIGHT?
WELL, NOW WE KNOW YOUR TRUE FEELINGS, SO THERE'S NO NEED TO BE DIFFICULT...
A PLAY?
SO, EVERY-THING WAS...
A LIE?
WELL, YES!
WE'VE ALL BEEN GETTING ALONG SO WELL TOGETHER,
WE'D NEVER GET IN A REAL FIGHT.

YEP.
I THOUGH YOU GUYS WERE FAKING
REALLY? HOW DID YOU KNOW?
WELL,
YOU DID SOUND LIKE YOU WERE READING FROM A SCRIPT.
YOU'RE SO SHARP, YUU!
YES, BUT IT WAS A GREAT SCRIPT.
SUPERVISION
YOU...
It was so much fun! I felt like an actress.
Too bad we lost that vase.
And we roke that cup, too.
SNAP
YOU IDIOTS ~~~!!

WAAAAH
WAAAAH
MIKI, DEAR?
BAM
BAM
MIKI!
WE'RE SO SORRY. THAT WAS WRONG OF US.
PLEASE, COME BACK OUT!
SHUT UP! GO AWAY! I HATE YOU!
WOW
I'VE NEVER SEEN HER THIS ANGRY...
MAYBE WE WENT TOO FAR?
I TOLD YOU WE SHOULDN'T HAVE DONE IT.
IT'S A LITTLE LATE FOR THAT NOW.
WE'RE ALL TO BLAME.

WHAT JERKS! THEY PLAYED WITH MY FEELINGS.
I CAN'T TAKE THIS ANYMORE!!
I'M LEAVING!!
IF I LEFT HOME NOW, WHERE WOULD I LIVE?
sniff
sniff
I COULD GO TO A PRIVATE SCHOOL OUT OF TOWN.
sniff
I'LL MAKE THEM PAY MY TUITION AND I'LL LIVE IN THE DORMS AND NEVER SEE THEM!
OH... BUT THEN I'D NEVER SEE MEIKO...
I don't want that.
Miki the Pragmatist
Knock
Knock
WHA!
HEY, MIKI!
OPEN UP!
PERVISION

WHA-
WHAT ARE YOU DOING...?
phew
POLO
HOW DID YOU GET HERE?!
I CLIMBED OVER FROM THE ROOM NEXT DOOR.
WHAT A RUSH! YOU SHOULD TRY IT.
YOU'RE KIDDING, RIGHT?
GASP
YOU'RE SO RECKLESS! WHAT IF YOU FELL? YOU COULD HAVE BEEN KILLED!!
YEAH, BUT AT LEAST YOU STOPPED CRYING.
....
I DID, DIDN'T I?
As a matter of fact...
HAHA
WHAT?
SOUNDS LIKE SHE'S TALKING TO YUU.
HUH?
HOW DID HE GET IN?!

THAT WAS PRETTY CRUEL OF THEM.
THIS TIME, THEY WENT TOO FAR.
blush
Don't they always?
THEY LIED TO YOU.
THAT'S NOT RIGHT.
YOU HAVE EVERY RIGHT TO BE MAD.
BUT,
OUR PARENTS...
THEY WERE CONCERNED THAT YOU DIDN'T REALLY MEAN IT WHEN YOU GAVE THEM YOUR OKAY.

ALL OF THIS WAS JUST THEIR WAY OF
MAKING SURE YOU DIDN'T HATE THEM FOR IT.
SO...
CAN YOU FORGIVE THEM?
EASE?
SUPERVISIO
NOD

OH, YUU.
I'M SO USED TO YOU BEING A JERK...
...THAT WHEN YOU'RE KIND AND GENTLE WITH ME...
...I DON'T KNOW WHAT TO THINK.

WE'RE SO SORRY.
FORGET ABOUT IT.
MIKI!
CLIC
BUT TOMORROW, YOU'RE GETTING ME WHATEVER I WANT FOR DINNER.
YEAH, YEAH.
FORGET ABOUT IT.
YOU REALLY SAVED US THERE, YUU!
squeeze
THANK YOU, MIKI!
WE'RE SORRY!
YUU...

DURING THE WHOLE CHARADE,
I WAS AFRAID I'D NEVER GET TO SEE YOU AGAIN.
I DON'T UNDERSTAND WHAT GOES THROUGH YOUR MIND.
AND SOMETIMES YOU CAN BE A REAL JERK.
BUT, SOMEHOW...
...YOU HAVE BECOME...
...AN IMPORTANT PART OF MY LIFE.

Summer Vacation
WHACK
(We still have practice during the summer.)
NICE SWING, KOISHI-KAWA.
YOUR SERVES ARE GETTING MUCH FASTER.
NOW WE JUST NEED TO WORK ON THAT ACCURACY...
I KNOW, I KNOW.
HUH?
YUU?!

WHAT ARE YOU DOING HERE?
YOU DON'T HAVE TO BE AT SCHOOL!
I CAME TO SEE YOU IN YOUR SKIRT.
WHAT?
BLUSH
YOU WISH! I'VE SEEN BETTER LEGS ON A CHAIR.
GRR...
WHAT A JERK!
Where did that kindness go?!

Ginta

BUT, REALLY...
WHY DID HE COME HERE?
FILA

KASHII Twin Towers
1989~
1 Model
2Plan and partial
YUU!
OH, HEY, MEIKO
I NEVER EXPECTED TO SEE YOU HERE.
NOT TOO MANY PEOPLE COME TO THE OLD LIBRARY.
LOOKS THAT WAY.
BUT, I DON'T MIND.
I LIKE OLD BUILD-INGS.
YEAH. ME, TOO.
IT'S SO QUIET AND PEACEFUL HERE.

YOU HERE FOR YOUR CLUB?
YEAH. IT'S ALMOST TIME FOR THE MEETING.
I GOT HERE EARLY, SO I THOUGHT I'D DO SOME RESEARCH.
LIT CLUB, RIGHT?
ARE YOU A WRITER?
NO, I DON'T WRITE.
I JUST READ A LOT!
RIGHT NOW, I'M DOING RESEARCH ON SOME OF MY FAVORITE AUTHORS.
WRITING ESSAYS FOR FUN?
impressive
NOTHING THAT FANCY.
I'M JUST PUTTING TOGETHER SOME PERSONAL NOTES.
LET ME TAKE A LOOK AT THEM SOME-TIME.
SURE!
SHOOM
Vol.24
Ripples
Quarterly magazine of the Toryo High Literary Club

THAT'L BE $5.00!
THANK YOU FOR YOUR PURCHASE!
......
We're saved! The club is so low on funds. If you like it, we have lots of back issues!
HEY,
MEIKO!
ARE YOU DONE FOR THE DAY?
LET'S GO HOME TOGETHER.
SURE!
LET ME GO CHANGE.
FILA

I JUST RAN INTO YOUR STEP-BROTHER AT THE LIBRARY!
YUU?!
THE LIBRARY?
WHAT WAS HE DOING THERE?
SO... HOW'S YOUR SUMMER VACATION GOING?
WHAT DO YOU MEAN?
WITH YOUR PARENTS AT WORK, YOU MUST BE SPENDING A LOT OF TIME WITH YUU.
ARE YOU GUYS GETTING ALONG?
WELL... TO BE HONEST,
WE REALLY DON'T SEE MUCH OF EACH OTHER.
I MEAN, I'VE GOT TENNIS PRACTICE,
AND YUU'S GOT A PART-TIME JOB, AND HE WENT OFF ON SOME TRIP...
WE ACTUALLY SEE LESS OF EACH OTHER NOW THEN WE DID WHILE WE WERE IN SCHOOL!
HMMM.

YOU SEEM DIS-APPOINTED.
SMILE
NO WAY!
IT'S NOT LIKE THAT!
YUU...
I WAS REALLY HOPING
TO GET TO KNOW HIM BETTER THIS SUMMER.
THERE'S SO MUCH ABOUT HIM I JUST DON'T UNDERSTAND.
HE NEVER TOLD ME WHERE HE WENT FOR HIS TRIP, AND HE DOESN'T TALK ABOUT HIS JOB.

ACTUALLY... MEIKO AND YUU ARE A LOT ALIKE.
THEY ALWAYS JUST SMILE AND NOD AND KEEP THEIR TRUE FEELINGS TO THEMSELVES.
WE'VE BEEN BEST FRIENDS SINCE STARTING JUNIOR HIGH,
BUT, I SOMETIMES FEEL LIKE I DON'T REALLY KNOW HER.
AH
WHAT AM I THINKING?!
COMPARING MY BEST FRIEND WITH THAT BASKET CASE?
FOOM
I'M SORRY, MEIKO!!
...FOR WHAT?

WONDER DOG?
ISN'T THAT THE NEW THEME PARK THAT JUST OPENED?
YUP!
My company's opening a restaurant in the park.
I GOT TWO FREE PASSES AT THE OFFICE.
YOU WANT 'EM?
WE'LL TAKE 'EM!!
YAY! I'VE BEEN DYING TO GO THERE!
COOL.
SOUNDS LIKE FUN.
THEY HAVE ALL KINDS OF GAMES AND RIDES AND JUNK FOOD, AND...
YOU GOT PRACTICE TOMORROW?
NO...
...
THEN LET'S GO.

UM...?
BAD DAY TO GO?
NO, NOT REALLY.
THEN IT'S SETTLED.
WONDER INVITATION
WONDER DOG
TONG TONG TONG
JUST THE TWO OF US?
THAT SOUNDS KIND OF LIKE...

...A DATE!
WONDER DOG
ZOOM
BOOM
ZOOOM
FUSUU
BOOM
BOOM
PIKUUM
V-GZOON
VROOM
BOOM
VOOM
WAAA!
HOW COME MINE WON'T HIT ANYTHING?
VOOM
BOOM
WHAT'S YOUR SCORE? YOU GOT A D?!
SHUT UP! I BET YOU DIDN'T DO MUCH BETTER.
You suck!
SCORE
I GOT AN A, LOSER.

LOOK, LOOK! THAT ONE'S SO KAWAII!
ISN'T IT CUTE?
YOU MEAN THAT ONE?
IT'S CUTE CUTE CUTE!
I WANT IT! I WANT IT!
STEP ASIDE AND LET THE MASTER HAVE A SHOT AT IT.
I'm good at these things.
HEE HEE
WISH HE
AS ALWAYS
IS SWEET!

HOO-YA!!
I GOT IT!
REALLY?!
......
THAT'S NOT IT!!
WHAT?
WASN'T THAT THE ONE YOU WERE POINTING AT?!
NOT THAT ONE! ARE YOU BLIND?!
squawk
squawk
.......

WELL, I GUESS I CAN GET USED TO IT... MAYBE.
I think I'll name it Kachan.
OOH, OOH! HALL OF MIRRORS!
LET'S GO IN THERE!
THE OL' HALL OF MIRRORS, EH? FOLLOW ME!
ENTRANCE
PULL!
?!
LONG TIME NO SEE, YUU.
ARIMI!

LOVELY KACHAN

PANIC
WAAA!
WHICH WAY'S THE EXIT?!
I'M SCARED! YUU!! WHERE ARE YOU?!
15 MINUTES LATER
FINALLY, SOME FRESH AIR!
EXIT
YUU!
HE GOT OUT BEFORE ME?
YUU...

HEY!
MIKI! OVER HERE.
WOW... SUCH A PRETTY GIRL.
A...
A FRIEND OF YOURS?
MIKI, THIS IS ARIMI SUZUKI. SHE'S AN OLD FRIEND FROM JUNIOR HIGH.
ARIMI, THIS IS THE GIRL I WAS TELLING YOU ABOUT, MIKI KOISHIKAWA. SHE'S KIND OF LIKE MY STEPSISTER.
SMILE
PLEASED TO MEET YOU.
YEAH... PLEASED TO MEET YOU, TOO...
WOW! SHE'S REALLY PRETTY.

SO, COULD YOU GIVE ME YOUR NEW ADDRESS AND TELEPHONE NUMBER?
SURE.
ADDRESS
WAIT!
HOLD ON A SEC.
AREN'T YOU TWO A LITTLE TOO COZY?!
ARIMI! AREN'T YOU DONE YET?
I'M COMING!
YOU'VE GOT A NEW BOY-FRIEND?
THAT'S COOL.

HE BEGGED ME TO GIVE HIM A CHANCE SO WE'VE GONE OUT A FEW TIMES.
HE'S NOTHING.
YOU WERE BETTER.
GRRR
BYE
I'LL CALL YOU SOON.
WHOA!
WOW.
SHE HASN'T CHANGED A BIT.
WHAT'S WITH THAT GIRL?!

WHAT DID SHE MEAN BY,
"YOU WERE BETTER"?
AH...
YOU KNOW, WE USED TO GO OUT.
OH.
HMMM...
SORT OF A
SHOCK
REALLY?
IT WAS ONLY FOR THREE MONTHS,
BUT WE DID PRETTY MUCH EVERY-THING.
E-
CLANG
A
B
C
EVERY-THING?!

YEAH,
YOU KNOW--
CHRISTMAS, NEW YEAR'S, VALENTINE'S DAY, BIRTHDAYS...
ALL THE THINGS THAT COUPLES DO TOGETHER.
OH...
YOU MEAN THOSE THINGS.
.....
WHAT, WERE YOU THINKING OF SOMETHING ELSE?
NO, I WASN'T!!
MIKI, YOU PERVERT!
WELL, SHOULD I TELL YOU HOW FAR WE WENT?
I WASN'T! REALLY!!
I DON'T WANT TO KNOW!!

WE DID NO-THING.
SUSPICIOUS
......
LIAR...
NO, REALLY.
MY FIRST KISS WAS YOU, MIKI.
PLAY BACK
YOU WERE AWAKE, WEREN'T YOU?
YOU KNEW ...?
NOT AT FIRST, NO.
BUT I FELT YOUR BODY MOVE WHILE I WAS DOING IT.
BLUSH

WH...
WHY...
WHY DID YOU DO THAT?
.....
WELL...
THE DEVIL MADE ME DO IT.
......
YIKES! I'M KIDDING!!
IT'S BECAUSE I LIKE YOU, MIKI.
!!
SLAP
STOP TEASING ME!!

YOU'RE ALWAYS MAKING FUN OF ME...
...AND YOU'RE NEVER SERIOUS WHEN WE TALK!
BUT, MIKI...
I DON'T CARE!
I'M GOING HOME!!
SMILE
I MADE HER MAD AGAIN.

GOOD MORNING GINTA.
Long time no see.
YO, MEIKO!
You go
a tan?
I went to the beach.
A DATE?! YUU AND MIKI?!
YUP,
I SAW THEM AT WONDER DOG.
I KNEW SOMETHING WAS GOING ON BETWEEN THEM!
I JUST KNEW IT!

WHAT'S MIKI DOING?
I THOUGHT SHE HATED YUU AND HIS STUPID FAMILY.
WHAT'S SHE SEE IN THAT IDIOT?!
HOLD ON, GINTA.
YOU HAVE NO RIGHT TO SAY THAT.
EVER SINCE THAT... INCIDENT, SHE'S HAD A HARD TIME GETTING CLOSE TO BOYS.
BUT NOW, I THINK SHE'S FINALLY STARTING TO FALL IN LOVE AGAIN.

AND YUU'S NOT SO BAD.
HE'S A LOT MORE MATURE THAN HE LETS ON.
I JUST WANT MIKI TO BE HAPPY, TO FEEL LOVE AGAIN.
GINTA...
YOU SEEM TO BE AWFULLY CONCERNED WITH HOW MIKI FEELS ABOUT YUU...
IT'S NONE OF YOUR BUSINESS!
I'M WARNING YOU, DON'T INTERFERE.

CLICK
GINTA,
DID YOU LOCK ALL THE WINDOWS?
YEP.
THEN ALL WE HAVE LEFT TO DO IS TO CHECK THE ATTENDANCE LOG.
IT'S SUCH A PAIN, HAVING TO DO CLEANUP SO SOON AFTER THE SEMESTER STARTS.
LOOK ON THE BRIGHT SIDE. AT LEAST IT'S A SHORT WEEK!
LET'S SEE, TODAY'S ABSENCES WERE SUZUKI...
ARIMI SUZUKI.
SHE CALLED SEVERAL TIMES.

SHE WANTS TO GET TOGETHER WITH YUU AGAIN.
YUU... WHAT WILL YOU DO?
I WONDER WHY THEY BROKE UP IN THE FIRST PLACE...
DID THEY GROW APART?
DID THEY FIGHT?
WE DID PRETTY MUCH EVERYTHING.
CHRISTMAS, NEW YEAR'S, VALENTINE'S...

New Year's
Birthday
Christmas
Valentine's

FUME
SUDDENLY ANGRY

MIKI?
WHAT'S WRONG?
Oh!
Your face is red.
AH! I'M SORRY. WHERE WERE WE?
AH, YES, TODAY'S NOTES.
Not much to write, is there?
HEY, MIKI.
WHAT'S THAT YOU'RE EATING?
OH, THIS?
IT'S A NEW KIND OF CANDY.
WANT ONE?
It's good.
Muscat Kiss
Riben
MUSCAT KISS? DOESN'T MIO HAGIWARA DO THE COMMERCIAL FOR THOSE?
THAT'S RIGHT.
THAT WAS A CUTE COM-MERCIAL.
Taste of a pure kiss.
Muscat Kiss.

TASTE OF A KISS...
I WONDER IF IT'S TRUE?
........
DOUBT IT.
I WAS SO SHOCKED, I COULDN'T TASTE A THING!
That time...
WANT TO FIND OUT?

HUH...?
GINTA?!

WANT TO FIND OUT?
........
WHAT ARE YOU SAYING, GINTA?

AH!
I GET IT.
HE'S JUST TRYING TO EMBARRASS ME.
You didn't think I meant it, did you?
Ha, ha, ha! Psych!
That's his plan.
I'M NOT FALLING FOR IT.
OKAY,
KISS ME.

Meiko

shoom
JUST KIDDING!
YOU KNOW, YOU SHOULDN'T TEASE ME LIKE THAT, GINTA.
...GINTA?
GRAB
WAAA!

BAM
STOP!!
HUFF
HUFF
HUFF
SLAP
WHAT ARE YOU DOING?!

OUCH....
WHAT'D YOU DO THAT FOR? YOU SAID IT WAS OKAY!
OF COURSE IT'S NOT OKAY, YOU JERK!
GINTA, YOU'RE SUCH AN IDIOT!!
tap tap
SLAM!

AH, CRAP.

I CAN'T BELIEVE IT.
WHAT WAS HE THINKING?!

WHY DID HE HAVE TO GO AND KISS ME?!
HE WOULD HAVE DONE THE SAME TO ANY GIRL!!
THE NERVE!!
HOW COULD HE?!
I'LL NEVER FORGIVE HIM!
RING
CLASS B
RING
RING
NEW ENGLISH 1
THAT'S IT FOR TODAY.
WE'LL FINISH COVERING THE PASSIVE TENSE TOMOR-ROW!

CLACK
YOU'RE GOING HOME ALREADY, MIKI?
I THOUGHT YOU HAD CLEANUP DUTY THIS WEEK.
TAG
HUH?
Do I have to do it now?
MIKI!
THERE'S SOMETHING I HAVE TO TELL YOU...
I DON'T WANT TO HEAR IT.

I DON'T EVEN WANT TO SEE YOUR FACE.
DON'T TALK TO ME!!
DASH
MIKI...
WHAT'S WITH THEM?
A FIGHT?
SOUNDS SERIOUS.
mumble
GINTA MUST HAVE DONE SOMETHING BAD.
mumble
HUH?
OH, NOTHING.

AH
GOOD AFTER-NOON.
BOW
ARIMI SUZUKI!

## FREE TALK⑥

You might be wondering why Miki and Ginta were cleaning up the classroom after school. Were they in detention? Not at all! In Japan, students are made to clean up classrooms starting in the first grade. In elementary school and junior high, all students pitch in every day to help with sweeping, cleaning chalkboards, and washing counters. In high school, some private schools hire janitors like most American schools, but some schools, like Miki's, still have the students clean and keep the class records.
- Editor

WHAT ARE YOU DOING?!
I'M WAITING FOR YUU...
SHH!
PLEASE, JUST PLAY ALONG!!
I haven't seen you in ages!
So, how have you been?
MI...
......?
Who was that?

phew
I GUESS HE STOPPED FOLLOWING ME.
YOU KNOW, YOU'RE SQUEEZ-ING MY ARM.
IT HURTS.
OH,
I'M SORRY!!
OOSH
SMOLDER
WOW, THAT'S NOT LIKE ME. I HARDLY KNOW THIS GIRL...
UM... UH...
THANKS FOR PLAYING ALONG. YOU DON'T KNOW HOW MUCH THAT HELPED ME.
WAIT!
shuffle
...AND HERE I AM, DRAGGIN HER ACROSS TOWN!
BOW
BOW
WELL... SEE YA!
HUH?
ARE YOU JUST GOING TO LEAVE ME HERE?
DID YOU PULL ME ALL THE WAY DOWN HERE FOR NOTHING?
WELL...
I... UH...

AS LONG AS WE'RE HERE, WHY DON'T WE STOP FOR SOME TEA?
I'VE BEEN WANTING TO TALK TO YOU, ANYWAY.
OF COURSE...
IT'S YOUR TREAT, RIGHT?
SURE...
MY TREAT...
DESSERT HOUSE
IN THAT CASE,
I'LL GET A DESSERT, TOO! ♡
nooo
SO...

WHO WAS THAT BOY?
WAS HE STALKING YOU OR SOMETHING?
UH...
NO... HE WAS A FRIEND.
WE JUST GOT IN AN ARGUMENT.
I SEE.
IS IT OKAY THAT YOU'RE HERE?
ISN'T YUU EXPECTING YOU?
DON'T WORRY.
HE ISN'T WAITING FOR ME.

HE HASN'T BEEN RETURNING MY CALLS,
SO I DECIDED TO SURPRISE HIM.
SO, ARE THE TWO OF YOU
GETTING BACK TOGETHER?
WHY DO YOU ASK?
HAS YUU SAID ANYTHING ABOUT ME?
HUH?
JUST THAT THE TWO OF YOU USED TO GO OUT...
THAT'S IT?
NOTHING ABOUT HOW WE GOT TOGETHER, OR WHY WE BROKE UP?
I GUESS
HE HASN'T TOLD YOU ABOUT IT...
SOUNDS LIKE YUU, ALRIGHT.
HE DOESN'T LIKE TO TALK ABOUT HIMSELF, DOES HE?

UH...
YEAH.
I KNEW IT.
SHE AND YUU WERE CLOSER THAN HE LETS ON...
IT'S NOT FAIR TO KEEP YOU IN THE DARK,
SO I'LL TELL YOU THE WHOLE STORY, OKAY?
I FIRST MET YUU IN THE 3RD YEAR OF JUNIOR HIGH.
WE WERE BOTH ON THE PLANNING COMMISSION FOR THE SCHOOL FIELD DAY.
I'D HEARD OF HIM, OF COURSE. HE WAS VERY POPULAR.

I DIDN'T CARE ABOUT HIM AT FIRST.
IT TAKES MORE THAN GOOD LOOKS TO INTEREST ME, AND BESIDES, THERE WERE PLENTY OF OTHER CUTE BOYS.
BUT WHEN I ACTUALLY TALKED TO YUU,
I FELL IN LOVE RIGHT AWAY.
I KNEW HE WAS THE ONE.
HE WAS SO MUCH FUN TO BE WITH!
SO, I TOLD HIM
HOW I FELT RIGHT AWAY.
THERE'RE PLENTY OF GUYS
WHO'D DIE TO GO OUT WITH YOU.
YOU DON'T WANT TO GO OUT WITH ME.
YES, I DO!
I DON'T WANT ANYONE BUT YOU.

I'M FLATTERED THAT YOU FEEL THAT WAY, BUT...
I'M NOT INTERESTED IN GOING OUT WITH GIRLS RIGHT NOW.
WHAT?!
I GUESS IT'S TRUE.
SO...
YOU ALWAYS TURN DOWN GIRLS THE SAME WAY.
IT'S OKAY.
I GET IT.
HOW MANY GIRLS HAVE HAD THEIR HEARTS BROKEN BY THAT ONE LINE?
IF YOU KNEW,
THEN WHY DID YOU...?

BECAUSE I'M CONFIDENT
YOU AND I ARE PERFECT FOR EACH OTHER.
GIVE ME THREE MONTHS.
THAT'S ALL THE TIME I NEED.
I KNOW YOU'LL SEE WHAT A PERFECT COUPLE WE ARE.
IF AFTER THREE MONTHS YOU DON'T THINK I'M YOUR DREAM GIRL,
I'LL JUST WALK AWAY AND NEVER BOTHER YOU AGAIN.
'KAY?
BUT...
CAN'T YOU JUST GIVE IT A TRY?
PLEASE! IT'S ONLY THREE MONTHS!!
THAT'S REASONABLE, ISN'T IT?

HEH
HA HA HA
YOU'RE REALLY DETERMINED,
AREN'T YOU?
I LOSE!
THOS WER THE BEST THRE MONTH OF M LIFE.
WE WENT OUT, WE HELPED EACH OTHER STUDY, WE TALKED ON THE PHONE...
WE REALLY HIT IT OFF.
I KNOW YUU HAD A GREAT TIME, TOO.
BUT...
THESE PAST THREE MONTHS HAVE BEEN GREAT,
AND YOU'RE A NICE GIRL...
BUT...

BUT...
I JUST CAN'T SEE YOU AS MORE THAN A FRIEND.
I'M SORRY...
WE WERE SO PERFECT...
ARIMI!!
IF IT CAN'T WORK OUT FOR US, THEN YOU'LL NEVER BE ABLE TO HAVE A RELATION-SHIP!
...PER-HAPS.

THE SHOCK... I WAS DEVASTATED.
BUT, C'EST LA VIE.
I HAD TO MOVE ON.
HIGH SCHOOL'S A NEW LIFE, RIGHT? I WAS DETERMINED TO FIND A NEW LOVE.
BUT, NO MATTER HOW HARD I LOOKED, I COULDN'T FIND ANYONE LIKE HIM.
AND THEN...
I RAN INTO YUU AT WONDER DOG.

I...
I JUST CAN'T FORGET.
EVEN NOW,
I STILL LOVE HIM.
HOW ABOUT YOU?
WHAT?
DON'T YOU LIKE HIM, TOO?
I'M NOT GOING TO LOSE.
SMILE

"I'M NOT GOING TO LOSE."
WHY SHOULD I CARE?
IT'S NOT LIKE HE'S MY BOYFRIEND...
SURE, YUU'S BEEN A MAJOR PART OF MY LIFE LATELY,
BUT THAT'S BECAUSE HE'S LIKE FAMILY.
I'M INTERESTED IN HIM
BECAUSE I DON'T UNDERSTAND HIM.
IT'S NOT LIKE
I LIKE HIM.

I DON'T...
...LOVE HIM...
huh
GINTA!!

EXCUSE ME, BUT YOU'RE BLOCKING MY GATE. PLEASE MOVE.
NO...
MOVE IT!!
I WON'T!!
oh!

LET'S GET THIS OVER WITH.
IF YOU'VE GOT SOMETHING TO SAY, SAY IT NOW!
PLEASE...
DON'T BE ANGRY WITH ME.
DON'T BE ANGRY?!
YOU'RE NOT GETTING OFF THAT EASY!!
I THOUGHT WE WERE JUST "FRIENDS."
IT COULD HAVE BEEN MORE-- I CONFESSED MY FEELINGS TO YOU YEARS AGO AND YOU REJECTED ME, REMEMBER?
YOU THINK IT'S EASY BECOMING JUST A "FRIEND" TO THE ONE WHO BROKE YOUR HEART? WELL, IT'S NOT! BUT, NOW I THINK THAT WE HAVE A VERY SPECIAL FRIENDSHIP TOGETHER.
WHY'D YOU HAVE TO GO AND RUIN IT...
...BY DOING OMETHING SO STUPID?

BE-
BECAUSE I...
LOOK, I KNOW YOU'RE A GOOD PERSON,
BUT I JUST CAN'T TRUST YOU!
TWO YEARS AGO, I WROTE YOU A VERY PERSONAL LETTER, AND YOU WENT AND SHOWED IT OFF TO ALL YOUR FRIENDS--
NO!!
THAT'S NOT HOW IT HAPPENED!
I WOULDN'T DO THAT!
AND BESIDES,
YOU'RE TO BLAME FOR THAT, TOO!
WHAT?!

ME? I'M TO BLAME?!
YEAH, I GUESS IT'S MY FAULT SINCE I NEVER SHOULD HAVE SENT YOU THAT LETTER IN THE FIRST PLACE, YOU JERK!
WILL YOU SHUT UP?
LISTEN!
THAT LETTER! WHERE DID YOU PUT IT?!
HUH?
IN YOUR BAG.
THERE WERE SOME COMICS IN THERE, SO I STUCK IT IN ONE OF THE BOOKS.
THOSE COMICS...
THEY WEREN'T MINE!
WHAT?!

THAT DAY..
...MY FRIENDS AND I WERE HANGING OUT AFTER SCHOOL, WHEN...
GINTA, YOU SEEN MY COPY OF JUMP? I WANT TO READ "ONE PIECE
Not in my desk.
OH, SORRY.
I FORGOT TO PUT IT BACK. IT'S IN MY BAG. GO AHEAD AND TAKE IT.
flip
HEY...
LOOK AT THIS!
IT'S A LOVE LETTER!

HEY, GINTA! LOOK'S LIKE MIKI HAS A CRUSH ON YOU!!
THERE WAS NO TIME TO STOP IT.
EVERY-ONE SAW IT.
IT WAS TOO LATE...
UM...
REALLY...?
shock shock shock
I WISH THAT...
THAT I COULD HAVE READ IT AT HOME, ALONE.
I WAS REALLY HAPPY...
...THAT YOU GAVE ME

YOU WERE?
BACK THEN, YOU TOLD THOSE GUYS THAT YOU THOUGHT OF ME AS JUST A GOOD FRIEND...
NO! THAT'S NOT HOW I FELT!
MAYBE YOU DIDN'T KNOW.
...BUT YOU WERE REALLY POPULAR WITH THE GUYS!!
HUH?
YOU WERE ALWAYS SO CHEER-FUL.
EVERY-ONE THOUGHT YOU WERE CUTE.
MY FRIENDS, YAMAZAKI AND SHIBATA... THEY CAME UP TO ME...

HEY, GINTA.
YOU AND MIKI SEEM PRETTY CLOSE.
THERE'S NOTHING-YOU KNOW-GOING ON BETWEEN YOU GUYS, IS THERE?
'CUZ, IF NOT, WE'D LIKE A LITTLE PIECE OF HER ACTION!
I DIDN'T WANT TO LOSE YOU TO THEM.
I PLANNED ON TELLING YOU HOW I FELT ABOUT YOU.
I JUST DIDN'T HAVE THE COURAGE TO MAKE ENEMIES OF THOSE TWO, SO I...
SO, I LIED.
AW, COME ON! WE'RE NOT LIKE THAT!
gosh
SURE, WE SPEND A LOT OF TIME TOGETHER SINCE WE'RE BOTH ON THE TENNIS TEAM,
BUT IT'S NOT LIKE I'D WANT TO GO OUT WITH HER!
ARE YOU SURE?
OF COURSE I AM!
MIKI'S TOO MUCH OF A TOMBOY FOR ME.
WELL, IF THAT'S THE CASE...

EVERYTHING I TOLD THEM WAS A LIE...
Heh, heh... yeah. I want someone more feminine.
...THAT DAY.
YOU DON'T ACTUALLY LIKE HER, DO YOU, GINTA?
SHE'S JUST LIKE A FRIEND.
RIGHT?
YEAH...

WHAT ELSE COULD I HAVE SAID?
I NEVER WOULD HAVE GUESSED...
...THAT YOU WERE RIGHT OUTSIDE THE DOOR, HEARING EVERY-THING...
I HURT YOU SO MUCH.
I THOUGHT IT WAS HOPELESS.
I CUT MY HAIR FOR YOU, BUT I KNEW THAT WASN'T ENOUGH.
I DIDN'T THINK I'D EVER BE ABLE TO EARN YOUR TRUST.
I WAS WRONG,
LYING TO YAMAZAKI AND THOSE GUYS.
I WAS SUCH A COWARD.
AND SO, I COULD NEVER TELL YOU HOW I REALLY FELT... UNTIL NOW.

MIKI...
I LOVE YOU.
I'VE LOVED YOU
ALL ALONG!!
TO BE CONTINUED...

IN THE NEXT ISSUE OF
Marmalade Boy

MIKI'S BOY TROUBLE SPILLS ONTO THE TENNIS COURTS IN THE SECOND VOLUME OF MARMALADE BOY. WHEN HOT-HEADED GINTA'S DOUBLES PARTNER IS INJURED, HIS RIVAL, YUU, IS THE ONLY ONE WITH THE SKILLS TO FILL IN. IT'S A BIG MATCH FOR BOTH PARTIES, AS THEY'RE PLAYING AGAINST GINTA'S COUSIN TSUTOMU, WHO ALSO HAPPENS TO HATE YUU FOR STEALING THE GIRL THAT HE LIKED IN JUNIOR HIGH! THINGS GET EVEN MORE HEATED WHEN YUU'S FORMER GIRLFRIEND, ARIMI, SHOWS UP AT THE COURT AND BECOMES AFFECTIONATE WITH GINTA TO MAKE YUU AND MIKI JEALOUS. CONFUSED? YOU WON'T BE ONCE YOU PICK UP THE MOST ADDICTING TEEN SOAP OPERA ON THE MARKET!

ON SALE NOW!

# kare kano

*his and her circumstances*

Story by Masami Tsuda

**Life Was A Popularity Contest For Yukino. Somebody Is About To Steal Her Crown.**

Available Now At Your Favorite Book And Comic Stores!

| Rank | Name | Class | Points |
|---|---|---|---|
| 1 | ??? | | |
| 2 | ??? | | |
| 3 | Tomohiko Ta | B | |
| 4 | Takumi S | A | |
| 5 | Mieko Ta | E | |
| 6 | Nijo Watanab | C | |
| 7 | Akemi Imafuku | | |
| 8 | Mizue Tanaka | | |
| 9 | Yuki Honj | | |
| 10 | Reiko Yokod | | |
| 11 | Hiroki Sato | | |
| 12 | Akira Oshima | | |
| 13 | Eri Yugawa | | |
| 14 | Aiko Yamag | | |
| 15 | Shogo Ka | | |
| 16 | Masami Ha | | |
| 17 | Mizuho On | | |

HEH HEH



品質第一公式商品 100% AUTHENTIC MANGA

T TEEN AGE 13+

www.TOKYOPOP.com

TOKYOPOP